Learn to Dance
Modern Jive!

Robert Austin and Claire Hilliard
of *le*JIVE

Published by Sigma Leisure – an imprint of
Sigma Press, 1 South Oak Lane, Wilmslow, Cheshire SK9 6AR, England.

British Library Cataloguing in Publication Data
A CIP record for this book is available from the British Library.

ISBN: 1-85058-602-0

Typesetting and Design by: Sigma Press, Wilmslow, Cheshire.

Printed by: MFP Design & Print

Cover Design: The Agency, Wilmslow.

Photographs: Cover photograph kindly supplied by the Berkshire Press Ltd.; all other photographs provided by the authors.

Acknowledgments

Thanks to: "Young" Terry McLeod and Andrew Matthews for their help with the photographs; Lyndsey Clegg for all her hard work; and all *le*JIVErs, past and present, for their support and help in making *le*JIVE one of the most successful dance organisations in the country.

Contents

Before you Begin . . .

What's in a name?

Modern Jive is unusual as a form of dance. Unusual in that few people recognise the name; even those who dance it on a regular basis often do not realise that they are dancing this style!

Modern Jive is one of the major new dances to have appeared in the latter half of the twentieth century. In the United Kingdom, it is probably the most popular social dance amongst the 20-40 age group. It's fun, stylish, easy to learn and incredibly popular – so why haven't more people heard of it? The main companies who teach Modern Jive and run events operate their classes under trademarked names – depending on where you live you've probably heard of leJIVE, Le ROC, CEROC or one of the many other similar names used by independent dance teachers. The reasons for this are historic: once one company trademarked their company name it was inevitable that others would follow suit and, before long, the generic name "Modern Jive" was lost in the confusion of registered trademarks[*].

---

[*] leJIVE, Le ROC and CEROC are trademarks. All trademarks are acknowledged.

Basic Principles

The Moves

Modern Jive consists of a series of moves or figures which, when combined, make up the dance. These may be walks, turns, spins or footwork patterns; they are pre-set and then put together in sequence on the dance floor, in time to the music.

Some dances consist of only a limited number of different moves. In ballroom dancing, for instance, most social dancers will only be familiar with a few moves in each dance style. A ballroom dancer will know several different dance styles, but footwork patterns and moves are confined to the specific dance such as the waltz, foxtrot or cha-cha-cha.

Modern Jive is different. It can be danced to a wide variety of music and, because of this broad approach, there is a huge number of possible moves and figures. At leJIVE, for instance, we carry a "Karma Sutra" of over 400 moves and variations that are constantly being increased and updated. As a new dance, it is still evolving and developing; the better dancers are looking at older dance styles and borrowing, stealing and incorporating these moves and figures into Modern Jive. This wide variety of moves means that Modern Jivers can create an improvised kaleidoscope of constantly changing movement on the dance floor in which no single dance will ever be repeated. Wow!

Does this mean you need to know 400 moves before you can start to dance Modern Jive? Certainly not! With only a handful of moves under your belt you can dance easily and confidently. If you have never danced Modern Jive before, practise the beginners' moves in this book and don't worry if you forget some of them. Gradually change the order in which you dance them, repeat moves if you get stuck and introduce new ones as you grow in confidence. In time you will find the beginners' moves become second nature and you will start to increase your repertoire by introducing more ambitious ones.

Enjoy the dance! The best dancers always look as if they are having fun. Remember that it's not what you do, it's the way that you do it. Don't fall into the trap of doing many moves badly, concentrate on getting the simple ones right. The worst dancers are never beginners, they are the dancers who concentrate on accumulating more and more moves but forget that it's the style that counts.

Lead and Follow

With all partner dances, someone needs to determine what move is going to happen next – otherwise, we call it wrestling! In dancing, it is usual that the man leads and the woman follows; Modern Jive is no exception. Yes, we know it's sexist but the girls can comfort themselves with the thought that it is the man's job not only to lead but to show off the girl's dancing abilities to best advantage.

Leading and following are skills that must be learned in order for the dance to work. Men must be decisive and assertive and learn the body language necessary; the girls must develop confidence in their partner and allow themselves to be led from one move to the next. Because the men have to learn the moves and the leading skills, it often takes them a little longer to pick up the dance than the girls. That's why a beginner girl can often dance with a more experienced male dancer almost immediately. For the men, however, this is almost impossible. But don't give up hope – once you've mastered the skill of leading, not only will you progress quickly, you will find that if you try other dances you will pick them up at a faster rate too.

It should be stressed that leading is not about heaving the girl about in a brutal fashion. It simply means that you are smoothly but firmly taking the girl through the moves that you wish to execute. Executing the moves – yes! Executing your partner – never!

Equally, following is not about docility – the girl needs to retain tension in her arms at all times to pick up the lead from the man and to be helped in her spins and turns. The exact amount of tension will vary from partner to partner to achieve the right balance, but this will come with practice.

Signals

A lead is the indicator a man gives to his partner as the dance is happening. For example, if the man uses his left hand to draw the girl into his side, the girl is moving as he is leading. Ninety-five percent of all moves are accomplished simply through these "as it happens" leads. Some moves, however, need a pre-arranged indicator, or signal, which both partners understand so that the lady knows what is going to happen the beat before it actually does. For instance, if the man wishes to go into a double-handed move, he will signal by offering his free hand to his partner the beat before the double-handed move is going to happen. The girl, seeing the offered free hand, will then take it on the required beat.

Signals are essential for certain moves to work and they operate alongside the man's lead, but they are no substitute for the lead itself. This is worth mentioning because, as Modern Jive is increasing in popularity, many inexperienced teachers are creating unnecessary signals for moves. They are developing dancers who cannot dance with others who do not attend those specific classes. This may be great for business – but not quite so great for the dancers or the dance.

Choreography

Modern Jive is a "freestyle" dance, by which we mean that the moves are combined in an improvised way to fit with the music being played. The man leads and the girl follows. We believe that the essence, fun and excitement of Modern Jive lies in this spontaneity. All the moves in this book are completely leadable, and likewise all the moves taught in leJIVE classes across the country have recognisable leads. Choreography (pre-planned routines) should be kept on the stage and not on the dance floor.

The Beat

Most dance styles were either created or evolved to fit the beat and bar structure of a certain type of music. The Waltz, for instance, is based on three-beat figures (moves) because the music itself follows a 1-2-3 rhythm. Swing dance is based on an eight-beat-per-figure pattern, because swing music follows that pattern. Later variations such as the Jitterbug, Rock 'n' Roll and Ballroom Jive look more complicated because they incorporate many six-beat figures, even though the music is four beats to the bar. However, two six-beat figures bring the dancer back into the bar structure after every three bars of the music. Most dancers from other styles are used to this formal way of dancing where figures and bars coincide. Modern Jive, however, breaks all these rules – the moves can have anything between 2 and 20 beats (sometimes in the case of complex wrap sequences even more). The dance can cross the bar structure of the music at any point.

Modern Jive also stresses the "on-beat" of the music, the beat to which you would clap your hands. Other earlier forms of jive dance emphasise the "off beat" as well as the "on beat" and are therefore limited to the beat structure of the music that coincides with the dance. To put this simply, fifties-style Rock 'n' Roll dancing can only really be danced to Rock 'n' Roll music. Modern Jive, on the other hand, can be danced to Rock 'n' Roll, but also to a wide variety of other music as well.

This is not to say that the bar structure of music is not important. The best Modern Jivers can dance perfectly in time with the rhythms, cadences and beat and bar structure of the music. But they are not limited by it and are, therefore, capable of greater improvisation and interpretation than is available in other partner dances.

In this book we will show you the number of beats it takes to accomplish each figure; occasionally, we will mention the "off-beat" – but only when it is necessary to do the move successfully. We also include within the beat count the 'initiation beat' – normally one beat at the start of a move – which helps you to count in a given move. When you start to combine the moves, you will find that this beat is dropped – don't worry about this, all will become clear!

Tension and Re-directed Momentum

Modern Jive is highly elastic. Without sufficient tension, the dance will not work. This is not to say that either partner should dance aggressively, but both the man and the woman should experience some degree of "pull" in order to accomplish the moves. Equally, many of the moves involve the man altering the line of movement of his partner and literally re-directing the momentum of the girl.

Spins, Turns and Swizzles

An intrinsic part of the jive 'look' is the turning of the girl both clockwise and anti-clockwise. There are essentially three types of turn in Modern Jive:

The Spin: in a spin, the girl turns without any contact with the man, the man will lead the spin but, as the girl rotates, there is no hand contact. The man will "collect" the girl at the end of the movement.

The Turn: when the girl turns, she remains in hand contact with the man, the man will lead the turn by lifting his hand and use his finger tips to help the girl round. An anti-clockwise turn is called a Return and is often used to correct the girl's balance and to complete a figure.

Swizzles: A swizzle is a supported spin. The girl is led in the same way as a spin but the man uses one of his hands to create a pivot point above the girl. The lead does not come from the raised hand but the lower hand (as opposed to a turn).

Dance Floor Etiquette

Etiquette may sound old-fashioned and a throw-back to the Victorian age. However, being aware of some simple basic rules keeps the dance fun and allows everyone to enjoy an evening's dancing.

Be aware of others on the dance floor. On a crowded dance floor constantly look around to see what space is available. If you have limited room, show respect for others on the floor and try to dance closer, within your own space. Wild kicks, jumps and large moves may lead to injury to yourself, your partner and other dancers – so show some respect.

Ask other people to dance. It is quite normal at a Modern Jive event for both men and women to ask each other to dance. This is not a pick-up joint: everyone is there to dance and have a good time. If you are new to the dance, the best way to improve is by "freestyling". Even if you only know a few basic moves, you will learn more in half an hour on the dance floor than in a whole evening of tuition.

Every expert was once a beginner. Sometimes, more experienced dancers will feel that they are "too good" to dance with beginners. Two minutes of your time spent dancing with a beginner can mean a lot to someone new to the dance. Men especially will find that dancing with beginners is a great exercise in developing a good lead and often leads to unexpected improvements in dance style. No-one is ever "too good" at Modern Jive and, who knows, the person you have just turned down may prove in the long run to be the best dancer there – and they may have long memories!

Don't assume the worst. Sometimes, people may not want to dance for a wide variety of reasons, they may be too tired, they may not like a specific track or they may have agreed to dance with someone else. Don't assume that if someone does turn you down for a dance that they are being rude or arrogant.

Turn people down gracefully. If you do not feel like dancing with someone then be polite; you are under no obligation to dance with everyone in the class and a rude word or abrupt tone can put people off the dance for good.

Use a deodorant. The better you get at Modern Jive, the more energy you will use. This is a great aerobic exercise but it has one side effect – sweat! Everyone gets hot and sweaty – if you don't, you're not doing it right. So use a deodorant – your best friend won't tell you, but we will. The biggest turn-off on the dance floor is that pungent smell of stale sweat. Wash before you arrive at the class and use a deodorant. You'll find that you get a lot more dances that way.

Helpful Hints

✳ Don't stare at the floor while you are dancing – this is, after all, a partner dance! Not only will it look much better if you look at your partner's face rather than your feet, it will also give you a better alignment or 'line'. If you find it embarrassing gazing into your partner's eyes, just look at the bridge of their nose!

✳ Try to always dance on your toes rather than your heels as this will mean you are more balanced – look at skiers and the stance they adopt! Unless, of course, the particular move you are doing involves going back on your heels or whatever, in which case this is fine!

✳ A common bad habit for the girl is to put her spare hand behind her back whilst she spins or turns. This means that as she comes out of the spin or turn, her hand is not available should the man want to take it. Similarly, should the man want to "break" a move and change it halfway through he is restricted in doing so because he cannot find the girl's hand to lead it!

✳ Try not to let your "free" arm flop about limply at your side. This does not look stylish. It is far better always to keep tension in your arms rather than let your arm look as if it's got nothing to do with the rest of your body!

Section 1:
Beginners' Routines

Routine 1
(beginner)

This routine is made up of the three most basic moves in Modern Jive:

Arm Jive

First Move

Push Spin

Arm Jive

The couple should start facing each other standing close together, double-handed. The girl's hands are resting in the man's hands at waist height. The stance should be relaxed with knees slightly bent, feet shoulder-width apart and weight on the toes ready to move!

1 On the first beat, the man pulls back with his right hand and pushes with his left. As he does so, he pivots on the balls of his feet to his right. The girl will automatically do the same, pivoting to her right.

2 On the second beat, the man now pulls back with his left hand and pushes with his right, this time pivoting to his left. Again, the girl does the same and pivots to her left.

Both should remember to keep their elbows tucked in and not leave them flapping about like chickens! Also try not to swing the arms up and down but keep the action smooth and the arms at waist height so that they move like pistons.

3 The man pulls back again with his right hand and pivots to his right, as the girl again pivots to her right.

Remember to keep the feet apart as you pivot or you will lose your balance. Don't try to do this move standing up straight – it looks much better if the knees are bent!

4 This time as the man pulls back with his left hand he raises it, taking it back above his left shoulder to prepare the girl for a turn.

5 The man pushes with his left hand, starting to turn the girl in a clockwise direction, taking his hand just above her head as he does so and letting go with his right hand.

The hands for the turn should be fingertip to fingertip, not gripping too tightly. This allows more flexibility and avoids coming out in awkward handholds.

6 The man keeps his hand just above the girl's head as she completes the turn, dropping his hand and stepping back as she comes round to face him.

All turns are clockwise and take two beats. Don't try to rush them, you have more time than you think. Men should be careful not to "sweep" their turns or "stir" their partners. Remember men you are dancing with a lady not a bowl of porridge! It is important for the man not to raise his hand too high or the girl will go off balance.

7 The man steps in ◀
to return the girl.
This time he
takes his hand
just above her
head and starts to
turn her in an
anti-clockwise
direction.

8 The man keeps ◀
his hand just
above the girl's
head as she com-
pletes the return,
dropping his
hand and step-
ping back as she
comes round to
face him.

Returns are always anti-clockwise and again take two beats. They are usually done to counteract a clockwise turn and stop the girl from getting dizzy.

Now you have completed the Arm Jive you may wish to run through this a few times before attempting the next move so that you are comfortable with it.

First Move

For this move, the
couple should start
facing each other,
standing   close
together. The man's
left hand holds the
girl's right hand at
waist height – don't
let the hands drift
too high or too low.

1 On the first beat the man makes a small semi-circle with
the hands to his left as he steps back to initiate the start
of the move.

> Most moves begin with this small semi-circle as you step
> back. It is the best way to ensure you both start on the
> same beat!

2 The man now
draws the girl
into his right
hand side, step-
ping forward as
she comes in
and placing his
right hand on
her waist. The
girl should put
her left hand on
the man's upper arm or shoulder. The man's left hand is
raised at shoulder level still holding the girl's right
hand. You are now in the "First Move position".

3 Using his left hand, the man pushes down and round in a line towards the girl's waist, to turn her out to the side. The girl should step back on her right foot as she is turned out. The man should keep his body position facing forward, (but certainly can turn his head to look at his partner if he wishes). The man keeps his right hand on the small of the girl's back.

4 The man steps back slightly, to give the girl room, as he brings her back round to face, taking his left hand back and above his left shoulder to prepare for a turn.
His right hand is still at the girl's waist on her back.

5 As with the Arm Jive, the man pushes with his left hand to start to turn the girl in a clockwise direction. He keeps the left hand just above her head, letting go with his right hand on her back.

6 As the girl completes the turn and comes round to face, the man drops his hand and steps back.

7 The man steps in to return the girl. Again, he takes his hand just above her head and starts to turn her in an anti-clockwise direction.

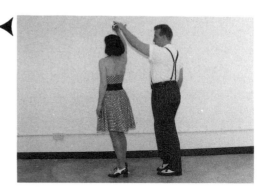

8 The man keeps his hand just above the girl's head as she completes the return, dropping his hand and stepping back as she comes round to face.

Practise this move on its own a few times to get used to it.

Now you have completed two simple moves, we need to link them so that you can begin dancing! Usually, when putting moves together, the small semi-circle at the start of each move is dropped.

So, having completed Beats 1 to 8 of the Arm Jive, you simply go into the First Move starting from Beat 2. This is because you are already in the "out" position, having stepped back and away from each other on completing the return.

Linking the Arm Jive to the First Move:

Arm Jive, Beat 8

The man keeps his hand just above the girl's head as she completes the return, dropping his hand and stepping back as she comes round to face him.

First Move, Beat 1 (previously 2)

As they are already in the "out" position, having just stepped back from each other, the man now draws the girl straight into his right hand side. He steps forward as she comes in, placing his right hand on her waist. The girl should put her left hand on the man's upper arm or shoulder. The man's left hand is raised at shoulder level still holding the girl's right hand. You are now in the "First Move position".

As you can see Beat 2 has now become the first beat of the First Move.

You should practise putting these two moves together until you are happy with the link between them.

Push Spin

For this move the ◀
couple should start
facing each other
standing   close
together, with the
man's left hand
holding the girl's
right hand at waist
height.

1 On the first beat the man makes a small semi-circle with
the hands to his left as he steps back to initiate the start
of the move.

2 The man now ◀
brings the girl for-
ward taking his
left hand back
and above his left
shoulder, flatten-
ing the hand in
preparation for a
spin.

The flat hand signals to the girl that the man is going to
push her on the next beat. The man takes his hand right
back above his shoulder. This enables him to give a full push,
rather than just raising his hand in front of his chest which
lessens the distance and force of the 'prepare'.

3 The man pushes down with his left hand in a smooth but firm line through the girl's shoulder, spinning her clockwise in front of him, stepping back slightly to give her room to spin.

The girl needs to make sure she has tension in her arm as the man pushes her, otherwise her arm will just flop to her side and this move will not work! Similarly, if the girl pushes back too hard the move will still not work and instead of spinning you will end up arm wrestling!

4 As the girl comes round to face the man catches her right hand with his left and they both step back.

5 The man steps in to return the girl, taking his hand just above her head and starts to turn her in an anti-clockwise direction.

6 The man keeps his hand just above the girl's head as she completes the return, dropping his hand and stepping back as she comes round to face.

Once you are happy with this move you can add it to the rest

of the routine. To do this you simply drop the first beat (i.e. the small semi-circle and step back) after the return on the First Move and begin the Push Spin from Beat 2.

Linking the First Move to the Push Spin:

First Move, Beat 8

The man keeps his hand just above the girl's head as she completes the return, dropping his hand and stepping back as she comes round to face him.

Push Spin, Beat 1 (previously 2)

The man now brings the girl forward taking his left hand back and above his left shoulder, flattening the hand in preparation for a spin.

As you can see, Beat 2 has now become the first beat of the Push Spin leaving out the small semi-circle and the step-back as you are already in the "out" position.

Practise all three moves in a sequence so that you are happy linking them together.

Linking the Push Spin back to the Arm Jive:

To complete the routine you need to take it back to the start of the Arm Jive so that you can dance all three moves continuously. To do this we will continue from Beat 6 of the Push Spin.

Push Spin

6 The man keeps his hand just above the girl's head as she completes the return, dropping his hand and step-

ping back as she comes round to face. As he steps back the man offers his right hand to the girl at waist height, letting her know that they are going into a double-handed move.

7 The man pulls the  girl in to face as she takes hold of his right hand so that they are now double-handed standing close together in front of each other. Remember to bend the knees and widen the stance slightly. This beat is a "check" beat so that both partners keep in time with the music and are ready to begin the Arm Jive again, like this:

1 The man pulls  back with his right hand and pushes with his left. As he does so, he pivots on the balls of his feet to his right. The girl will automatically do the same, pivoting to her right.

Now continue with the Arm Jive and repeat the sequence of moves . . .

Congratulations! You can now dance Modern Jive!

With just these three moves you can look fantastic on the dance floor and impress all your friends! That is, if you now go away and practise!

Once you are happy with this routine you can move on to the other routines in the book, adding more moves to your repertoire. Don't worry, men especially, if you can't remember all of them immediately. This will only come with time – even the most experienced dancers forget moves and need reminding sometimes!

The important thing is to have fun and enjoy the dance. Men: you should go away and dance just these three moves all evening with every girl in the room. By the end of the evening you will have met lots of new people. Nobody watching will know you were only doing three moves and you will have perfected this routine! What more can we say! (Girls, you should also dance with many different partners to practise "following" their lead.)

Routine 2
(beginner)

This routine will show you how to change places, how to change hands and another simple spin.

Shoulder Slide

Right-Handed Comb

Step-Across Man Spin

American Spin

Shoulder Slide

The couple should
start facing each
other standing close
together, with the
man's left hand
holding the girl's
right hand at waist
height – remember
not to let the hands
drift too high or too
low.

1 On the first beat the man makes a small semi-circle with
the hands to his left as he steps back to initiate the start
of the move. There should be plenty of tension between them.

2 On the second
beat, the man
draws the girl for-
ward, as he steps
across, taking her
hand up on to his
right shoulder
and "latching" it
there as they
cross each other.

3 The man lets go
with his left hand
as he continues
to step across. He
lets the girl's arm
slide down and
across his back,
turning to face
her as they come
out, having

changed places. He catches with his right hand as they
both step back.

> This move looks better if the girl lets her hand slide across
> the man's back rather than pulling it away as soon as he
> relaxes his grip. Obviously, a sweaty back is not ideal but is
> often a reality so sometimes the girls just have to grin and
> bear it!

4 The man steps in to
return the girl, ex-
actly the same as
before but this time
using his right hand.
He takes it just
above her head as
he starts to turn her
in an anti-clockwise
direction.

5 The man keeps his hand just above the girl's head as she
completes the return, dropping that hand as she comes
round to face and stepping back.

> At the end of this move the man will have changed places
> with his partner so that they are still facing each other but
> now the other way round.

Repeat this move several times so that it begins to flow.

Right-Handed Comb

This time, the couple start standing close together, facing each other with the girl's right hand resting in the man's right hand.

1 On the first beat the man makes a small semi-circle with the hands to his right as he steps back to initiate the start of the move.

The small semi-circle this time is to the right because it is a right-handed move. It always goes in the direction of the hand leading it.

2 The man now steps in towards his partner, still facing her, taking her right hand up over his head and placing it at the back of his neck.

The most common fault with this move is that the man ducks his head or hunches his shoulders as he takes his hand over his head. So, to make this move look more stylish, especially if you are taller than your partner, bend your knees as you step in. Widening the stance will also help keep your balance. Remember to always lose height from your knees, never from your head or shoulders.

3 The man lets go of the girl's hand as he steps back, letting it slide down his arm to catch with his left hand. Again, girls beware of sweaty necks!

There is no need to put in a return after a Comb because the girl hasn't gone anywhere. Returns are nearly always corrective and are used after a clockwise spin or turn to stop the girl getting dizzy.

Practise the Comb on its own a few times. The men especially need to get used to bending their knees and keeping their heads upright. This move looks even better if you look at your partner as you do it, not the floor!

Now it's time to put the two moves together:

Coming out of the return from the Shoulder Slide you will be in the "out" position right-to-right-handed. The man leads the girl straight in taking the hand up over his head and leaving it on the back of his neck. When part of a routine, the Comb is just a two-beat move.

Practise these two moves together and then try the next move.

Step-Across Man Spin

This is another left-handed move, so start off close together with the man's left hand holding the girl's right hand.

1 On the first beat, the man makes a small semi-circle with his hand to his left as they step back. At this point, the man has his right arm slightly raised, away from his side, ready for  the next beat, but not taking the arm straight out. This is *not* a signal.

2 The man now wraps himself in towards his partner (turning himself anti-clockwise), drawing her across behind and taking his right arm up so  that it skims across his left arm.

> The reason the man raises his right arm is to stop it getting trapped at his side as he wraps himself in. It looks far smoother to take the arm over the top of the other one as the man steps across.

3 The man lets go with his left hand as they change places, letting the girl's hand slide round his back. As he does this, he turns to face her  and catches her right hand again with his left. They are now facing each other but have changed places and the man is standing where the girl started.

4 The man steps in to return the girl, taking his hand just above her head and starts to turn her in an anti-clockwise direction.

5 The man keeps his hand just above the girl's head as she comes round to face, dropping his hand and stepping back as she completes the return.

You have now completed another move enabling you to change places with your partner. Practise this move on its own before adding to the previous two.

Remember: you do not need to do a return after the Comb. As the man steps back out of this move, he should have his right arm ready to raise across his left as he wraps himself straight in to the Step-Across Man Spin.

You can now put all three moves together into a routine.

American Spin

We will add one more move to complete this routine before taking it back to the start. This time, it's a spin. The couple should start facing each other standing close together, with the man's left hand holding the girl's right hand at waist height.

1 On the first beat, ◄ the man makes a small semi-circle with the hands to his left as they step back and away from each other.

2 On the second ◄ beat, the man draws the girl forward and across in front of him. He takes the hands across to his right-hand side, leading the girl into a 'p r e p a r e'

position. The girl steps forward on her right foot – choosing a spot on which to spin. The man should keep the hands low at the girl's waist height.

There should be tension in the girl's arm for this move to work. It helps if the girl balls her hand into a fist which will give her automatic tension in her arm and gives the man something to push against. The man can also flatten his hand to push hers.

3 The man pushes across with his left hand to spin the girl clockwise, keeping the lead smooth and firm and not pushing up or down.

4 As the girl comes ◀ round to face, the man catches her right hand with his left hand and they step back.

5 The man steps in to return the girl, taking his hand just above her head and starts to turn her in an anti-clockwise direction.

6 The man keeps his hand just above the girl's head as she comes round to face, dropping his hand and stepping back as she completes the return.

You have now completed the final move in this routine. Again, practise this move on its own a couple of times before attempting the whole routine.

Linking the moves

To put it all together – once you have stepped back out of the return from the American Spin you are ready to go straight back to the top of the routine. The man draws the girl across as he wraps himself straight in to the Shoulder Slide, latching her hand on his shoulder.

Having put the whole routine together, you can repeat it as many times as you like! Now put some music on and try dancing the moves a little faster.

Congratulations! You have now completed two routines. You can mix and match the moves you have learned so far, adding the four new ones to your repertoire.

Routine 3
(beginner)

This routine will show you some right-handed moves, how to change hands and another simple spin.

Yo-Yo

Half Catapult

Lady Spin

Left-Handed Comb

Yo-Yo

This is the first move
in the routine. The
couple should start
facing each other
standing   close
together, with the
man's right hand
holding the girl's
right hand at waist
height.

1   On the first beat the man makes a small semi-circle with
the hands to his right as he steps back to initiate the
start of the move.

2   On the second
beat, the man
draws the girl for-
ward to his right
hand side, as he
takes his right
arm   up   and
across his chest
towards his left
shoulder.

They are now facing opposite directions. At this point the
girl should not turn in towards the man to put her left
hand on his shoulder but remain facing forward with her left
arm at her side.

3 The man takes his right arm straight out to the side turning the girl out behind him. She should step back on her right foot and now place her left hand on the man's right shoulder for balance.

If the girl takes her left arm up to the man's shoulder too soon it spoils the whole line of this move. Men should be careful not to lean across to the side and drop their arm as they turn the girl out, but should keep their right arm straight, at about shoulder level.

4 The man takes a step back as he brings the girl back round to the front to face, blocking forearm to forearm. The girl steps round on her right foot, pivoting on her left.

It is very important that the man steps back to give the girl room as he brings her round to face, otherwise she will have a very long distance to travel.

5 The man pushes with his right hand to start to turn the girl in a clockwise direction, taking his hand just up above her head.

6 The man keeps his hand above her head as she comes round to face, dropping the hands and stepping back.

7 The man steps in to return the girl, taking his hand just above her head and starts to turn her in an anti-clockwise direction.

8 The man keeps his hand just above the girl's head as she comes round to face, dropping his hand and stepping back as she completes the return.

Repeat this move several times. The next move is the Half Catapult.

Half Catapult

The couple start standing close together, facing each other with the man's right hand holding the girl's right hand.

1 On the first beat the man makes a small semi-circle with the hands to his right as he steps back to initiate the start of the move.

2 The man steps forward, pulling straight down with his right hand and begins to sweep that arm up as he draws the girl through.

3 Continuing the sweep, as the girl comes under his arm, the man steps past the girl on his right foot. He leans forward, stretching his left arm out to the front and

clicks his fingers on the third beat. The girl is now behind the man and there should be plenty of tension between them as the man leans forward.

Girls should try to keep their shoulders back and not let their bums stick out! This move has got a really nice line, especially if the man bends forward on his right leg and keeps his left leg straight behind. The lower he can get, the better it looks! How low can you go?!

4 The man steps back as he starts to sweep his arm back up, pulling the girl back through towards the front.

5 Continuing the sweep, the man brings the girl back out to face, dropping the hands, as they step back and away from each other.

The man must keep his arm high as he brings the girl back through to the front so that he does not hit her head as she moves under his arm. Girls should try not to duck their heads!

There is no need to put in a return after the Half Catapult.

Practise the Half Catapult on its own a few times. The men especially need to get used to bending their knees, clicking their fingers and keeping their heads up — all at the same time! This move looks better if you look up and not at the floor!

Putting the two moves together:

Coming out of the return from the Yo-Yo you will be in the "out" position still right-to-right-handed. The man pulls straight down with that right hand, sweeping it up as he steps forward leading the girl behind for the Half Catapult.

Practise these two moves together and then try the next move.

Lady Spin

This is another right-handed move, so start off close together with the man's right hand holding the girl's right hand.

1 On the first beat the man makes a small semi-circle with the hands to his right as they step back. At this point the girl should automatically be back on her right foot as she came out of the last move.

2 The man draws the girl across taking the hands over to his right hand side, keeping them low, at the girl's waist height. The girl should step across on her right foot, pick-  ing a spot on which to spin. This is called a 'prepare'.

> For this move to work there needs to be tension in the arms for both the man and the girl. Ideally the girl should ball her hand into a fist and the man will flatten his palm ready to push the girl into the spin.

3 The man pushes across with his right hand in a straight line, keeping it level with the girl's waist to spin her in a clockwise direction.

> The lead needs to be a firm push from the man but not too aggressive – keep it smooth! The girl needs to push back

slightly – but remember not too much or you'll turn it into a
wrestling match!

4 As the girl comes
round to face,
the man catches
her right hand
with his left hand
and they step
back and away
from each other.

5 The man steps in to return the girl, taking his hand just
above her head and starts to turn her in an anti-
clockwise direction.

6 The man keeps his hand just above the girl's head as she
comes round to face, dropping his hand and stepping
back as she completes the return.

You have now completed the third move in the third routine!

Adding this on . . .

As the man brings the girl out of the Half Catapult to face, you
will be in the "out" position still right-to-right-handed. Remember there is no need for a return. The man then draws the hands
across in front of him straight into a prepare for the Lady Spin.

**As you can see, spins are useful moves for when you want to
change hands. Another useful move to change hands is a
'comb' – and that comes next!**

Left-Handed Comb

As you can guess, this is a left-handed move, so start off close together with the man's left hand holding the girl's right hand .

1 On the first beat, ◀
the man makes a
small semi-circle
with the hands to
his left as they
step back and
away from each
other.

2 On the second ◀
beat, the man
steps in towards
the girl, turning
sideways on so
that his left shoul-
der is nearer the
girl. As he does
this, he takes her
hand up and over
his head, placing
it on his right shoulder.

The man should bend his knees as he steps in for this move
(as for the Right-Handed Comb). Don't duck your head.
Turn to your right as you step in but be careful not to lean
across – keep the back and shoulders straight.

3 The man lets go ◀
with his left hand
and steps back
letting the girl's
hand slide out as
he turns back to
face her full on to
catch with his
right hand.

You may wish to repeat the Left-Handed Comb a few times before adding it to the routine, especially as it differs from the
earlier Comb.

Dancing the whole routine . . .

Now, let's put the whole routine together. Having stepped back
out of the Left-Handed Comb and caught with the right hand,
the man is ready to draw the girl straight in to his side, taking his
right arm up across his chest into the Yo-Yo.

Try the whole thing to some slow music. When you feel confident, you can speed it up!

With these first three routines you now have plenty of moves
to stun all your friends on the dance floor. You do not need
thousands of moves to look good – fewer moves done cor-
rectly will always reveal the better dancers! However, if you
want to expand and improve your repertoire, move on to the
next set of routines.

Section 2:

Improvers' Routines

Routine 4
(Improver)

This routine will show you variations on some of the previous moves.

Travelling Arm Jive

First Move Spin

Man Step Under

Travelling Return

Travelling Arm Jive

The first move in the routine is the Travelling Arm Jive. The couple should start facing each other standing close together, with the man's left hand holding the girl's right hand at waist height.

1 On the first beat the man makes a small semi-circle with the hands to his left as he steps back to initiate the start of the move. As he does so, he offers his right hand to his partner, indicating that this is a double-handed move.

2 On the second beat, the man pulls back with his left hand, bringing the girl into his right hand side as she takes hold of his right hand.

As for the standard Arm Jive, the arms should be kept at waist height and the elbows tucked in – not swinging up and down. They should ideally move like pistons.

3 The man pulls with his right hand and pushes round with his left taking the girl out as he steps round to face her, so that they have changed places. Again, keep the elbows tucked in. They are now in an "out" position.

This move looks a lot better if the man bends his knees and adopts a wider stance.

4 As before, the man pulls back with his left hand, bringing the girl back in to his right hand side.

5 The man pushes round again with his left hand, pulling back with his right as he steps round to face, again taking the girl out to the front and changing places.

6 To come out of
the move, the
man steps in to
bring the girl
straight in to-
wards him. He
takes his left
hand back and up
above his left
shoulder, in
preparation for a
turn.

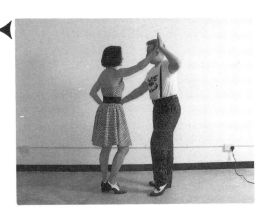

7 The man starts to
turn the girl, tak-
ing his hand just
above her head,
in a clockwise di-
rection.

8 Keeping his hand
above her head
as she continues
to turn, dropping the hands and stepping back as she
comes round to face.

9 The man then steps in to return the girl, again taking his
hand just above her head and starts to turn her in an
anti-clockwise direction.

10 The man keeps his hand just above the girl's head until
she comes round to face and then drops the hands and
steps back as she completes the return.

**Repeat this move, remembering to keep the arms from swing-
ing and the elbows from flapping!**

First Møve Spin

Here's the second move in this routine. The couple start standing close together, facing each other with the man's left hand holding the girl's right hand.

1 On the first beat the man makes a small semi-circle with the hands to his left as they step back.

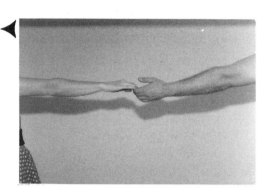

2 The man now draws the girl into his right hand side, stepping forward as she comes in and placing his right hand on her waist. The girl should put her left hand on the

man's upper arm or shoulder. The man's left hand is raised at shoulder level still holding the girl's right hand. You are now in the "First Move position".

3 Using his left hand, the man pushes down and round in a line towards the girl's waist, throwing her hand away as he turns her out to the side. The girl should step back on her right foot as she is turned out. The man should keep his body position facing forward, with his right hand on the small of the girl's back.

4 The man steps back slightly to give the girl room, as he brings her forward, using his right hand on her back to guide her. The girl should step forward on her right foot.

5 Again using his right hand on the girl's back the man pushes the girl, spinning her out to the front.

6 As the girl comes round to face the man catches her right hand with his left hand.

The spin for the girl can either be a half spin to the front or, if she wishes, she can make it one and a half spins! It is best to start with the half spin until you are happy with your spins and then progress to one and a half when you feel more confident.

7 The man then steps in to return the girl, again taking his hand just above her head and starts to turn her in an anti-clockwise direction.

8 The man keeps his hand just above the girl's head until she comes round to face and then drops the hands and steps back as she completes the return.

Joining the two moves . . .

Repeat this move a few times before adding it to the Travelling Armjive, like this: coming out of the return from the Travelling Arm Jive, you will be in the "out" position, left-to-right-handed. The man draws the girl straight in to his right-hand side into the First Move position.

Practise these two moves together and then try the next move.

Man Step Under

This is another left-handed move, so start off close together with the man's left hand holding the girl's right hand.

1   On the first beat the man makes a small semi-circle with the hands to his left as they step back.

2   The man raises his left arm as he walks forward under that arm, drawing the girl across.

The men need to bend their knees to lose height and keep their heads up – not look at the floor – as they step under their arm, rather then hunch their shoulders. Many men often lean backwards as they go under. Again, try to avoid this – it does not look cool! This is yet another move that looks better the lower the man gets!

3   As the man goes past the girl, he turns to face and drops his hands, signalling the end of the move. This ensures that the girl also turns to face and does not continue travelling past him.

This move has only three beats, so you can try this a few times to get it looking right.

Linking the move:

Here's how to add it to the rest of the routine: the man, having completed the return after the First Move Spin, draws the girl straight forward, raising his left hand as he steps under.

Travelling Return

This is the final move in this routine. It is a left-handed move, so start off close together with the man's left hand holding the girl's right hand.

1 On the first beat ◀ the man makes a small semi-circle with the hands to his left as they step back and away from each other.

2 On the second ◀ beat, the man simply draws the girl forward, leading with his left hand just slightly above and in front of her head, as he steps forward too.

It is important that the man does not try to turn the girl at this point but should just let her walk forward.

3 As the girl walks forward, she will get so far until she cannot walk any further and will automatically turn herself out to face (either that, or her arm will drop off!) They will have both now changed places.

Men will often be tempted to turn the girl out but this will only mean they lose the beat and draw the girl off balance. A Travelling Return may be used at any time to replace a standard return.

Adding the Travelling Return . . .

To add that to the Man Step Under, you simply drop the small semi-circle to the left as you are already in the "out" position; the man just leads the girl forward for the Travelling Return.

To repeat the routine from the beginning, the man must offer his right hand to the girl as soon as he steps back out of the Travelling Return. She will then know that the next move is going to be a double-handed move.

Try this routine to music, repeating it through several times. This will get the men used to signalling a double-handed move.

Practise all the moves you have learned so far in freestyle, mixing them up so that the men can improve their lead and the girls get more accomplished at following it.

Routine 5
(Improver)

This routine includes moves with signals and double-handed moves:

Neckbreak

Hatchback

Catapult

Basket

Neckbreak

This is the first move in the routine. The couple start facing each other standing close together, with the man's left hand holding the girl's right hand at waist height.

1 On the first beat the man makes a small semi-circle with the hands to his left as he steps back to initiate the start of the move. As he does so, he takes his right arm up and holds it at right angles to his shoulder. This is the signal for the Neckbreak.

2 On the second beat, the man draws the girl straight in to his right hand side, raising his left hand up to his left shoulder. He should take care not to garrotte his partner as he brings her forward! At this point, the man rests the heel of his right hand gently on the girl's left shoulder. They are both facing opposite directions.

3 The man turns
the girl out to the
side by changing
her right hand
into his right
hand, keeping
his arm resting on
her shoulders.
The girl should
step back on her
right foot, keep-
ing her left arm at her side

Girls are sometimes tempted to put their left arm around
the man's back as he turns her out. However, this makes it
more difficult for the man to bring her back in on the next
beat and is uncomfortable for the girl.

4 Still with his
arm across her
shoulder the
man guides the
girl back to the
front as she steps
forward   on
her right foot,
stepping back
slightly as he
does so to give
her room.

If the man lets his right arm come up off the girl's shoulder
it means he will have less control over his partner and not
be able to lead the move properly

Try to keep this move open so that the man does not crush
the girl by bringing her in too close. This move may be called
a Neckbreak but don't take it literally! The girls should keep
their heads up and shoulders back. (Deodorant is definitely
advised for this move!)

5 The man now
pulls back slightly
with his right
hand before rais-
ing it just above
the girl's head to
turn her out. It is
one and a half
turns for the girl.

6 As she comes
round to face,
the man drops
the hands and
steps back.

7 The man then steps in to return the girl, again taking his
hand just above her head and starts to turn her in an
anti-clockwise direction.

8 The man keeps his hand just above the girl's head until
she comes round to face and then drops the hands and
steps back as she completes the return.

**Repeat this move. The man must remember to signal as soon
as he steps back. The Neckbreak is a hand change move so
you will have now come out right-to-right-handed.**

Hatchback

The couple start standing close together, facing each other with the man's right hand holding the girl's right hand.

1   On the first beat the man makes a small semi-circle with the hands to his right as he steps back to initiate the start of the move.

2   On the second
beat, the man
draws the girl for-
ward to his right
hand side, step-
ping forward as
he takes his right
arm up and
across his chest
towards his left
shoulder.

They are now facing opposite directions. So far, this move
is identical to the Yo-Yo.

3   Leading with his
right shoulder,
the man throws
his right arm
down and across
to the side, step-
ping forward on
his right foot as
he spins the girl
behind him.

4 As he does so the
man step spins to
face the girl,
catching her right
hand with his
right hand as she
completes the
spin and steps
back.

The difference
between the Hatchback and the Yo-Yo comes from the
man's lead. For the Yo-Yo the man takes his right arm
straight out to the side, keeping hold of the girl's hand
turning her out behind. With the Hatchback the man throws
his hand down and across to the right, following through
with his right shoulder as he spins the girl behind.

5 The man then steps in to return the girl, again taking his
hand just above her head and starts to turn her in an
anti-clockwise direction.

6 The man keeps his hand just above the girl's head until
she comes round to face, and then drops the hands and
steps back as she completes the return.

**Practise the Hatchback a few times so that the man can get
used to the difference in lead.**

Putting the Neckbreak and the Hatchback together . . .

. . . coming out of the return from the Neckbreak you will be in
the "out" position, right-to-right-handed. The man then steps in
drawing the girl straight in to his right hand side taking his arm up
across his chest into the Hatchback.

Practise these two moves together and then try the next one:

Catapult

This is another right-handed move, so start off close together with the man's right hand holding the girl's right hand.

1   On the first beat the man makes a small semi-circle with the hands to his right as they step back.

2   On the second beat, the man pulls straight down with his right hand in a bowling action, as he steps forward, drawing the girl through under his arm.

3   Continuing the sweep up with that arm he takes the girl out behind and has his left hand ready, offered to the girl behind his back. As she comes through she

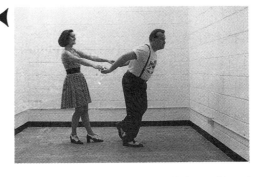

takes hold of the man's left hand with her left hand and they check in this position. The man should be pulling forward and the girl should be pulling back, taking care not to let her bum stick out but keeping her shoulders back. There should be plenty of tension between them at this point. The man needs to keep his head up and not stare at that spot on the floor!

4 The man takes a step back and to his right as he brings the girl across to his left hand side. At this point he should keep his left hand low – at the girl's waist height – in preparation for a spin.

5 The man steps back as he pulls back with his left hand to spin the girl in a clockwise direction to the front.

6 As the girl comes round to face he catches her right hand with his left hand and steps back.

It is vital that the man moves around the girl, stepping backwards and forwards to give her room as she moves. If the man does not move, the girl then has a far greater distance to cover and the move will be uncomfortable. By simply stepping forward and back to accommodate the girl, it will look as if the girl has still travelled the same distance but it will feel and look a lot smoother.

7 The man then steps in to return the girl, taking his hand just above her head starting to turn her in an anti-clockwise direction.

8 The man keeps his hand just above the girl's head until she comes round to face and then drops the hands and steps back as she completes the return.

Add the Catapult to the other two moves . . .

Coming out of the Hatchback the man has caught the girl with his right hand before returning her. Having stepped back from the return he is then ready to pull straight down with that right hand, as he steps forward, drawing the girl through behind him for the Catapult.

Again, in freestyle the man can catch with whichever hand he chooses, depending on what move he plans to take his partner in to next.

Basket

This is the final move in this routine. It is a double-handed move, but we will start with a left-to-right hold so that the man can lead it.

1 On the first beat the man makes a small semi-circle with the hands to his left as they step back and away from each other. As he steps back, he offers his right hand to his partner.

2 On the second beat, the girl takes hold of the man's right hand with her left hand. He wraps her in to his right hand side by raising his left hand and turning her anti-clockwise,

keeping his right hand low. The man now has the girl wrapped into his side with his left hand holding her right at the front. You are now in the "Basket position".

> Try not to have the hands at the front too high, too low or tucked in too close but in a comfortable arc with the arms bent.

3 The man pulls ◀ back with his right hand to draw the girl into a sway, stepping back on her right foot as he sways back on his right foot.

The weight should remain on the right foot rather than letting the weight fall onto the left foot which will mean you lean forward and lose the line of the move. Remember to keep the toes pointing down!

4 The man brings the girl back to the front, pulling her forward with his left hand, so that she steps forward on her right foot.

5 Raising his left ◀ hand, the man starts to turn the girl clockwise, unwrapping her to the front.

6 As she comes round, the man drops the hands and they step back to face, still double-handed.

This turn-out takes two beats, so don't try to rush it and complete it in one as you will end up sweeping the turn and losing the beat.

7 The man lets go ◀ with his right hand and steps in to re- turn the girl, taking his left hand up just above her head as he starts to turn her in an anti-clockwise di- rection.

8 As the girl comes round to face, the man drops the hands and they step back.

Linking the Catapult to the Basket

As the man steps back out of the return from the Catapult he needs to have his right hand ready. He offers it to the girl so that she knows they are going into a double-handed move. He can then wrap her straight into his right hand side on the next beat, raising his left hand as he turns her anti-clockwise, into the Basket position.

To repeat the routine from the top . . .

The man must signal clearly to the girl with his right hand at right angles to his shoulder when he steps back out of the return from the Basket. She then knows that the next move is going to be a Neckbreak. He can then draw her straight into his side, resting the heel of his hand on her shoulder ready to turn her out and continue the rest of the routine.

It is very important that the man signals as soon as he steps back from the previous move to let the girl know what move is coming next – otherwise there is no point having a signal!

Try this routine to music, repeating it several times. Keep the music playing and try adding some of the moves from previous routines to mix and match!

There is one more routine to do in this Improvers' section.

Routine 6
(Improver)

This routine will look at "travelling" variations on some of the moves covered so far.

Sway

Travelling Yo-Yo

Travelling Lady Spin

First Move Push Spin

Sway

Start close together, with the man's right hand holding the girl's right hand.

1   On the first beat the man makes a small semi-circle with the hands to his right and steps back.

2   On the second 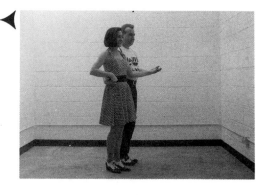 beat, the man pulls straight down with his right hand wrapping the girl into his right hand side. His right hand should be palm upwards at the girl's hip. Her right hand should be resting on his with her fingers curled under, similar to a dog's paw! The man also picks up the girl's left hand in his left hand at the front.

> The lead for the Sway needs to be a very firm – but not rough – pull down from the man. Wimpy men need not attempt this! The man should not try to pull out to the side, but keep the pull straight down to wrap the girl in – it works, honest!

3   The man pulls back with his right hand to draw the girl into a sway, stepping back on her right foot. He should also sway back on his right foot. As for the Basket, keep the weight on the right foot, not on the left, to maintain the line and try not to lean forward. Keep the toes pointing down.

This move looks better (and sexier) if the couple look at each other as they sway back. You can even smile! Remember this is partner dancing!

4 The man brings the girl back forward, using his right arm at her back to guide her, so that she steps in on her right foot.

5 To turn the girl out, the man gives a small push with his left hand and lets go. By simply raising his right hand straight up in the air the girl will automatically start to turn in a clockwise direction.

6 Taking his hand to just above her head until she comes round to face, the man then drops the hands and steps back.

It is important that the man does not try to turn the girl. This is uncomfortable for the girl and it will not be a smooth turn. Instead he should simply raise his hand until it reaches just above the girl's head and she will turn automatically – try it, it works!

7 The man then steps in to return the girl, again taking his hand just above her head and starts to turn her in an anti-clockwise direction.

8 The man keeps his hand just above the girl's head until she comes round to face and then drops the hands and steps back as she completes the return.

Repeat this move, remembering that the man must pull straight down to wrap the girl in and push straight up to turn the girl out. You will have come out of this move still right-to-right-handed so you are ready for the Travelling Yo-Yo:

Travelling Yo-Yo

Start close together, man's right hand to girl's right hand.

1 On the first beat the man makes a small semi-circle with the hands to his right as they step back.

2 On the second beat, the man draws the girl forward to his right hand side, stepping forward as he takes his right arm up and across his chest towards his left shoulder.

They are now facing opposite directions. So far this move is identical to the standard Yo-Yo.

3 As the man takes his right arm straight out to the side, turning the girl out behind, he steps round to face, so that they are now in the "out" position having changed places. The girl should step back on her right foot.

The difference between this and the standard Yo-Yo is that the man steps round to face his partner as he takes his right arm out to the side. The girl does not put her left hand on the man's shoulder either as she is not able to do so – she is too far away!

4 The man draws
the girl back in to-
wards him, step-
ping forward to
block forearm-
to-forearm.

5 The man then
pushes with his
right hand and
raises it just
above the girl's head to start to turn her in a clockwise
direction.

6 The man keeps his hand just above the girl's head until
she comes round to face and then drops the hands and
steps back.

7 The man then steps in to return the girl, again taking his
hand just above her head and starts to turn her in an
anti-clockwise direction.

8 The man keeps his hand just above the girl's head until
she comes round to face, then drops the hands and
steps back as she completes the return.

**Practise the Travelling Yo-Yo to differentiate the lead from the
standard Yo-Yo.**

Adding the Travelling Yo-Yo to the Sway . . .

Coming out of the return from the Sway you will be in the "out" position, right-to-right-handed. The man then steps in drawing the girl
straight in to his right hand side taking his arm up across his chest
into the Yo-Yo.

**Practise these two moves together, then try another travelling
move:**

Travelling Lady Spin

This again is a right-handed move, so start off close together, man's right hand to girl's right hand.

1 On the first beat the man makes a small semi-circle with the hands to his right as they step back. The girl should automatically step back on her right foot.

2 On the second beat, the man draws the girl across to his right into a prepare position, as he steps forward. He keeps his hands low at the girl's waist

height. The girl should step across on her right foot as for a standard Lady Spin.

> At this point the girl is at the man's side. The man can flatten his hand against the girl's. The girl should have tension in her arm ready for the spin. The difference between the Travelling Lady Spin and the standard Lady Spin is that the man steps forward to the girl's side for the prepare in the travelling version.

3 The man now spins the girl behind, keeping the lead smooth and across (not up or down), as he steps round to face.

4 The man catches the girl's right hand with his left hand and steps back.

They have now changed places.

5 The man steps in to return the girl, taking his hand just above her head and starts to turn her in an anti-clockwise direction.

6 The man keeps his hand just above the girl's head until she comes round to face, then drops the hands and steps back as she completes the return.

Add the Travelling Lady Spin to the other two moves . . .

Coming out of the Travelling Yo-Yo the man has still got hold of the girl's right hand with his right hand. The girl will be back on her right foot. The man draws the girl across to the right, as he steps forward, into the prepare position.

In freestyle, the man can catch with whatever hand he chooses, depending on what move he plans to take his partner in to next.

First Move Push Spin

This is the final move in the routine. It is a left-handed move, so start off close together, man's left hand to girl's right hand.

1 On the first beat the man makes a small semi-circle with the hands to his left as they step back and away from each other.

2 On the second beat the man steps forward drawing the girl into his right hand side, so they are hip-to-hip! He places his right hand on her waist. The girl places her left hand on the man's upper arm.

3 The man pushes down and across towards the girl's waist with his left hand as he turns her out to the side. The girl should step back on her right foot.

4 The man steps back slightly to give the girl room as he brings her back round to face, leading with his left hand. The girl should step back round on her right foot. As he  does so, the man takes his left hand back and above his left shoulder, flattening it in preparation for a spin.

The flat hand is a signal to the girl that she is about to be pushed.

5 Relaxing the hold with his right hand, the man pushes down with his left, in a line through the girl's shoulder, to spin her clockwise to the front.

6 As she comes round, the man catches her right hand with his right hand and they step back.

Don't forget, in freestyle the man can catch with either hand, depending on which move he wants to go into next.

7 The man steps in to return the girl, taking his left hand just up above her head and starts to turn her in an anti-clockwise direction.

8 As the girl comes round to face, the man drops the hands and steps back.

That's the last move for this routine (and for this section)!

Linking from the Travelling Lady Spin . . .

Coming out of the Travelling Lady Spin the man has caught the girl's right hand with his left hand. After returning her, he is in the "out" position to then draw her straight in to the First Move position.

Try the whole routine, from the top . . .

The man has caught the girl's right hand with his right hand after the First Move Push Spin. He then returns her and steps back. They are now in the "out" position in a right-to-right hand hold. He can then pull straight down with that right hand to wrap the girl into his side for the Sway. Continue the routine as before.

Time for some music!

You have now completed all the moves in the improvers' section and by now you should be looking really good on the dance floor!

Section 3:
Intermediate-level Routines

Routine 7

(Intermediate)

This routine features some variations on some of the earlier moves and another way of changing hands.

Hatchback Combo

Nelson Accordion

Overhead Hand Change

Basket Spin

Hatchback Combo

For the first move in the routine, start close together, man's right hand to girl's right hand.

1 On the first beat the man makes a small semi-circle with the hands to his right and steps back.

2 On the second beat, the man draws the girl into his right hand side, taking his right arm up straight across his chest to his left shoulder.

The couple should now be hip-to-hip, facing in opposite directions.

3 The man throws his right arm out and down to the side, stepping forward as he does so, to spin the girl behind him.

Unlike the Hatchback the man does not step spin to face the girl but remains facing forward.

4 The man offers his right hand behind, as he now has his back to the girl, who catches that hand as she comes out of her spin.

The man should not look round behind him at his partner as this will move his hand away from her. The girl can see the man's hand straight in front of her and so she will catch it!

5 The man steps back and across to his right, changing the girl's right hand from his right hand to his left, so that the girl is now at his left hand side. The

man should keep the hands low at this point (at the girl's waist height) as he prepares to spin the girl.

6 As the man flick spins the girl clockwise to the front, keeping his hand at the same level, he takes a step back to give her room.

This step back for the man is vital, ensuring that the girl can spin much more smoothly as he gets out of her way. Many men try to sweep the spin and not move their feet. However, this is not comfortable for the girl: she is having to travel a greater distance which the man could easily shorten, making this a much sharper move. After all men, it's your job to make the girl look good!

7 As she comes round to face, the man catches her right hand with his right hand and they step back.

8 The man then steps in to return the girl, taking his hand just above her head and starts to turn her in an anti-clockwise direction.

9 The man keeps his hand just above the girl's head until she comes round to face and then drops the hands and steps back as she completes the return.

As you can see, that was a combination of the Hatchback and the Catapult. Now you've completed the Hatchback Combo you can try another right-handed move.

Nelson Accordion

Start close together, man's right hand to girl's right hand.

1 On the first beat
the man makes a
small semi-circle
with the hands to
his right as he
steps back to ini-
tiate the start of
the move. As he
steps back, the
man offers his
left hand behind
his back signalling to the girl that he will be taking her
into a Nelson.

> There are many variations on the Nelson and at this point
> the girl does not know into which one they are going. She
> will have to wait for the man to lead it!

2 On the second
beat, the man
draws the girl for-
ward to his right
hand side, taking
his right arm up
across his chest
towards his left
shoulder.

> At this point the girl will be tempted to take hold of the
> man's left hand behind his back. RESIST! As soon as the
> girl does this she spoils the whole line of the move. Instead
> she should wait for the man to turn her out.

3 The man takes  his right arm straight out to the side turning the girl out behind him, who now takes hold of his left hand behind his back with her left hand. They should now be double-handed.

If the man wishes, as he takes his right arm out he can cross-step, so that his left foot steps in front of his right. This is not obligatory, but it makes the next part of the move a lot easier!

4 Keeping hold  with his left hand behind his back, the man starts to turn anti-clockwise under his right arm, transferring the weight onto his left foot to turn. As he comes round to face the girl, he dips his right hand on the "and" beat before . . .

5 . . . turning the girl clockwise.

6 As she comes
round to face,
they step back
and should still
be   double-
handed with left
hands over right.

The left hands
should remain
high and not be
allowed to drop together with the right hands below.

7 The man pulls
with his right
hand (the lower
one) to draw the
girl across, as he
steps across too
behind her.

8 As they come
back out to face,
they now have
the right hands raised over the left.

9 This time the
man pulls with
his left hand
(which is now the
lower one) to
draw the girl
back across, as he
again   steps
across behind
her.

10 As they step back ◄ out to face, they now have the left hands raised over the right again.

The Accordion
can be repeated as often as you like. Remember to keep the hands apart and not to let them drift together in the middle as this does not look so good.

Adding this on:

Coming out of the return from the Hatchback Combo you will be in the "out" position, right-to-right-handed. At this point, the man needs to signal with his left hand behind his back – letting the girl know they are now going into a Nelson.

Practise this, making sure that the man gives a good clear signal!

Overhead Hand Change

There are many ways to come out of an Accordion, however, one of the more usual ways is with an Overhead Hand Change. This is a double-handed move, so start from the Accordion position with the left hands over the right.

1 The man starts to ◄ turn the girl anti-clockwise in front of him leading with his right hand, raising it as he turns her.

2 As she comes ◄ round to face he drops the hands and they both step back, now in a cross-handed hold.

You can now take this into the Overhead Hand Change . . .

3 The man steps in towards his partner, drawing her forward and taking their hands straight up above their heads.

4 When the hands reach the top, the man changes them over. He then steps back, sweeping the hands down in an arc out to the sides to come out facing with a double-handed  hold (but no longer cross-handed).

Add this to the other moves and then try the final move in this routine . . .

Basket Spin

This is the final move in this routine and it's a double-handed move. You are already in the "out" position holding with both hands.

1 Keeping his right hand low, the man raises his left hand. Stepping forward slightly, he turns the girl anti-clockwise to wrap her into his side, so that they are hip-to-hip. He should let the

arms drop to about waist height at the front in a comfortable arc.

Be careful not to leave the hands up high. The lead for the sway back comes from the man's right hand pulling the girl, not his left pushing her back.

2 The man pulls with his right hand to draw the girl back so that they both sway back on their right foot, letting the weight go onto that foot.

If the weight goes onto the left foot you will end up leaning forward and losing the line of this move. Try to keep the

toes pointing down: a foot waving around in the air will also break the line! This is another move when looking at your partner really improves it!

3 The man brings the girl forward, keeping his left hand low. She should step forward on her right foot.

4 The man lets go with his left hand and pulls with his right to spin the girl to the front. He should keep the pull as firm and smooth as possible, trying to pull neither up nor down but straight across.

5 As the girl comes round to face the man catches her right hand with his right hand and they step back

Don't forget: in freestyle the man can catch with either hand, depending on which move he wants to go into next.

6 The man steps in to return the girl. He takes his right hand up just above her head and starts to turn her in an anti-clockwise direction.

7 As the girl comes round to face, the man drops the hands and they step back.

That's the last move in this routine.

To go back to the beginning:

Coming out of the return after the Basket Spin they are now in the "out" position in a right-to-right-hand hold. The man can then draw the girl straight in for the Hatchback Combo, taking his right arm up across his chest.

Now try the whole routine to some music!

You have now completed your first Intermediate routine. You can mix and match all the moves you have learned so far and should be feeling a lot more confident out on the dance floor.

The only way to get good at this dance is to keep practising! Good luck.

Routine 8
(Intermediate)

This routine again features variations on some of the moves covered earlier in the book.

Travelling First Move

Half Neckbreak

Half Windmill

Octopus

Travelling First Move

The first move in this routine is another variation on the First Move. Start close together, man's left hand to girl's right hand.

1 On the first beat the man makes a small semi-circle with the hands to his left and steps back.

2 On the second beat the man steps forward drawing the girl into his right hand side, so they are hip-to-hip! He places his right hand on her waist. The girl places her left hand on the man's upper arm.

3 The man pushes down and round with his left hand, turning the girl out. As he does so, he follows round to face – pivoting on his right foot as he takes a big step round on his left foot. (This can be quite a big step!) The man should keep his right hand on the girl's back at all times. His left hand is also low at waist height, still holding the

girl's right hand. The girl should step back on her right
foot.

*This move looks better and is a lot more comfortable
(especially for the girl!) if the man bends his knees and gets
quite low as he steps round to face. The man should also
remember to keep his feet apart, otherwise he may fall over!*

4 The man then
starts to take the
girl into a return,
taking his left
hand up above
her head as he
turns her anti-
clockwise, re-
leasing hold with
his right hand.

5 As the girl comes
out of the return
the man drops
the hands and
they step back.

*There is no full
clockwise turn with
this move as with
a standard First
Move because they
have already turned as they changed places.*

**Practise this, remembering that the man must bend his knees!
The next move is another variation – this time on the Neckbreak.**

Half Neckbreak

Start close together, man's left hand to girl's right hand.

1 On the first beat the man makes a small semi-circle with the hands to his left and steps back. As he steps back, he signals with his right arm – holding it at right angles to his shoulder. This  lets the girl know that they are going into a Neckbreak.

> It is important that the man signals as soon as he steps back, otherwise the girl will not be able to react to his signal. As we have said before, the whole point of a signal is to let your partner know what is about to happen next!

2 On the second beat, the man draws the girl straight in to his right-hand side. He raises his left hand up to his left shoulder, taking care not to gar- rotte his partner as he brings her  forward. At this point the man rests the heel of his right hand gently on the girl's left shoulder. They are both facing opposite directions.

3 The man turns the girl out to the side by changing her right hand into his right hand keeping his arm resting on her shoulders. The girl should step back on her right foot, keep-  ing her left arm at her side out of the way.

4 Still with his arm across her shoul- der, the man guides the girl back to the front as she steps for- ward on her right foot. He steps back slightly as he does so to give  her room. At this point the man should place his left hand on the girl's left shoulder – this is the signal for a Half Neckbreak as opposed to a standard one.

Some men feel they need to put their left hand on the girl's shoulder during a standard Neckbreak. This will only confuse the girl and is unnecessary for that move, unlike the Half Neckbreak when it is an important signal to differentiate between the two moves.

5 In one beat, the ◀
man pulls back
with his right
hand and pushes
the girl's shoul-
der with his left
to take her
straight out to the
front, dropping
the hands as they
step back.

This is a very fast turn out for the girl. You have been
warned!

**Practise the Half Neckbreak, especially the signals, then add it
to the Travelling First Move . . .**

Stepping back out of the return from the Travelling First Move
you will be in the "out" position, left-to-right-handed. At this
point the man should signal with his right arm at right angles to
his shoulder, letting the girl know the next move is a Neckbreak,
before pulling her straight forward to his side.

Practise these two moves together and then try the next one.

Half Windmill

This is a right-handed move, so start off close together with the man's right hand holding the girl's right hand.

1 On the first beat the man makes a small semi-circle with the hands to his right as they step back.

2 On the second beat, the man pulls straight down with his right hand, sweeping his arm up, pulling the girl through behind, turning to his left as he does so. They should 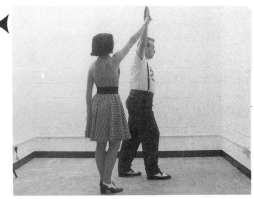 both now be facing the same direction with the girl behind the man.

3 Bringing his right arm straight down behind his back the man passes the girl's hand into his left hand, changing hands exactly on the 3rd beat.

4 Continuing the ◀
sweep upwards
with his left arm
the man brings
the girl back
through to face
and steps back.

The motion for the man is just raising and lowering his
arms, keeping them straight and changing hands at the
bottom of the arc. If there is a big difference in height
between the two, the arms should still remain straight and
the distance between them then varies.

Add the Half Windmill to the other two moves . . .

Coming out of the Half Neckbreak the man has now got hold of
the girl's right hand with his right hand. He can then pull straight
down, leading the girl forward and through behind, as he
sweeps his arm up.

Oₑₜₒpus

This is the final move in this routine. It's a double-handed move but we will start off with the man's left hand to girl's right hand, so that it can be led in freestyle.

1 On the first beat the man makes a small semi-circle with the hands to his left as they step back and away from each other. As he does this he also offers his right hand to his partner, let-ting her know this is going to be a double-handed move.

2 On the second beat the girl takes the man's hand as he raises his left hand to draw her across, stepping behind her as she comes through.

3 The man lets go with his right hand as they come out to face, having changed places and catching double-handed as they step back.

This first part of the move – the first three beats – is called a Girl Breakthrough. The next part is a Man Breakthrough . . .

4 The man steps in, raising his right hand as he wraps himself in. He has now stepped across in front of the girl.

5 He lets go with his left hand continuing to step across as they come out to face, having changed places once again and catching double-handed as they step back.

To complete the Octopus, you need to add another Girl Breakthrough...

6 The man raises his left hand drawing the girl through stepping across behind her as she comes across.

7 The man lets go
with his right
hand as they
come out to
face, having
changed places
and stepping
back. This time
the man does
not catch again
with his right
hand but remains in a left-to-right-hand hold.

That's the last move for this routine.

Completing the sequence:

Coming out of the Half Windmill the man has now got hold of the girl's right hand with his left hand. At this point he should offer his right hand to his partner to let her know the next move is going to be a double-handed move. He can then draw the girl across for the Girl Breakthrough.

To repeat the routine, when you come out of the Octopus you should be left-to-right-handed, ready to go straight into the Travelling First Move. Continue the routine as before.

Time for some music!

There is one more routine to go in this Intermediate section.

Routine 9
(Intermediate)

In Modern Jive many moves can be "travelled", so that you're not just dancing in one small area. This routine features more variations, including one that enables you to travel around the room.

First Move Walk

Open Neckbreak

Lassoo

Back Comb Flick

First Move Walk

Start close together, man's left hand to girl's right hand.

1 On the first beat, the man makes a small semi-circle with the hands to his left and they both step back.

2 On the second beat, the man draws the girl into his right hand side, placing his right hand on her waist as she puts her left hand on his upper arm.

3 The man pushes down and across with his left hand to turn the girl out to the side. She should step back on her right foot, the man steps back on his left.

The man can now alter the whole look of this move depending on which foot he steps back on. In this instance the man will step back on his left to "mirror" what the girl is doing.

4 The man steps
forward on his
left foot, pulling
the girl forward
with his left
hand, keeping it
low, as she steps
forward on her
right foot. The
man should also

use his right hand on the small of the girl's back to help
guide her forward.

They are both stepping forward on their outside feet and
turning towards each other.

5 The man pushes
across with his left
hand, still with his
right hand on the
girl's back. He
uses this to guide
her, as they each
step forward on
their inside foot
(man's right foot,

girl's left), this time turning away from each other.

6 The man pulls
again with his left
hand to draw the
girl forward as
they step on their
outside feet once
more (man's left,
girl's right), turn-
ing towards each
other.

7 The man pushes
with his left
hand, as they
step forward
again on the in-
side feet (man's
right, girl's left)
turning away
from each other.

The man uses his left hand to push/pull and guide the girl
as they walk forward. His right hand stays at the small of
her back as additional support. This move can be walked all
around the room if desired by just repeating steps 4 to 7.

If the man stepped forward on his right foot first – i.e. the
same foot as the girl – they would lose the turning towards
and away from each other and the move would look
completely different. This is fine, however, as the footwork
for the girl remains the same!

To come out of the walk . . .

8 The man leads
the girl back in to
a standard First
Move position.
He steps back
slightly as she
steps in on her
right foot, bring-
ing her round to
face and taking
his left hand
back above his shoulder.

9 The man then raises his hand just above the girl's head to start to turn her in a clockwise direction.

10 The man keeps his hand just above the girl's head until she comes round to face and then drops the hands and steps back.

11 The man then steps in to return the girl, again taking his hand just above her head and starts to turn her in an anti-clockwise direction.

12 The man keeps his hand just above the girl's head until she comes round to face and then drops the hands and steps back as she completes the return.

You can repeat this move as often as you like. It is very useful for when you spot that empty corner of the dance floor just across the room!

The next move is another Neckbreak variation . . .

Open Neckbreak

Start close together, man's left hand to girl's right hand.

1 On the first beat, the man makes a small semi-circle with the hands to his left and steps back. As he steps back, he takes his right arm straight out horizontally to his side, level with his shoul-

der. This is the signal for the Open Neckbreak.

2 On the second beat, the man draws the girl forward to his right hand side, with his arm straight across in front of her.

They are now facing opposite directions. The man needs to be careful not to garrotte his partner.

3 The man takes
   the girl's right
   hand and places
   it in his right
   hand as he starts
   to turn her. At
   this point the
   man also starts to
   step round to
   face the girl,
   keeping his right
   arm resting on her shoulder.

4 The man contin-
   ues the turn for
   the girl, pulling
   back with his
   right hand and
   starting to raise it
   to just above her
   head as she
   turns.

   *It is important
   that the man
   does not raise his hand too soon as he turns the girl, but
   waits until she comes round from the first turn.*

5 As she comes round to face again he drops the hands
   and steps back, having now both changed places.

**Practise the Open Neckbreak although be careful not to get
too dizzy as we have not put on a return yet! Add the move to
the First Move Walk . . .**

Coming out of the return from the First Move Walk you will be in
the "out" position, left-to-right-handed. At this point the man
needs to signal to his partner that they are going into an Open
Neckbreak, taking his right arm straight out to the side.

Practise these two moves together and then try the Lassoo!

Lasso

This is a right-handed move, so start off close together with the man's right hand holding the girl's right hand.

1   On the first beat the man makes a small semi-circle with the hands to his right as they step back.

2   On the second ◄ beat, the man steps in, raising his right hand to return the girl, and starting to turn her anti-clockwise.

3   As the girl comes ◄ round to face, the man pulls straight down with his right hand, drawing her into his right hand side. He picks up the girl's left hand with his left hand. The man's right hand is palm up at the girl's hip, with her right hand curled under (like a dog's paw) resting on his.

4 The man draws the girl back, pulling with his right hand so that they both sway back on the right foot.

The weight should go back on the right foot, keeping the toes pointing down, to give a better line. If the weight is on the left foot, you will end up leaning forward which does not look so good.

5 The man takes the girl back forward so that she steps back in on her right foot.

6 Letting go with his left hand and by just raising his right hand straight up, the girl starts to turn out (as for the Sway). The man should take care not to raise his hand too high, but to just above the girl's head.

7 As the girl comes round to face the man drops the hands and they step back.

As with the Open Neckbreak, we will not add on a return at this point.

Add the Lassoo to the other two moves . . .

Coming out of the Open Neckbreak the man has still got hold of the girl's right hand with his right hand. At this point they have not added a return. The man starts to take the girl into the return but as she comes round to face he pulls straight down wrapping her into his side.

Back Comb Flick

This final move is another right-handed one, so start off close together, man's right hand to girl's right hand.

1 On the first beat the man makes a small semi-circle with the hands to his right as they step back and away from each other.

2 On the second beat the man steps in, raising his right hand to return the girl, starting to turn her anti-clockwise.

3 As the girl comes round to face the man turns himself clockwise under his own arm to rest his right hand (still holding the girl's hand) on his right shoulder. He now has his back to the girl.

4 The man lets
go of the girl's
hand and steps
forward, letting
the girl's hand
slide down his
back to catch
with his right
hand behind. He
still has his back
to his partner.

The man should
not look round at his partner to check she will catch his
hand. If he does, he will hinder the move because this takes
his hand away from the girl's grasp. So the man must
remember to remain looking forward – but not at the floor!
Heads up!

5 The man takes his
hand across be-
hind his back,
turning to his left
to prepare.

6 The man flick
spins the girl
clockwise be-
hind him as he
spins clockwise
to face.

Try to keep the
flick smooth and
at an even level.

7 As they both come round to face, the man catches the girl's right hand with his left hand and they step back.

8 The man steps in to take the girl into a return, raising his left hand as he starts to turn her anti-clockwise.

9 The man keeps his hand just above the girl's head as she completes the turn. He then drops his hand and they both step back.

That's the last move for this routine (and for this section)!

Completing the Routine . . .

The man has still got hold of the girl's right hand with his right hand after the Lassoo and they are in the "out" position. The man steps in to take her into a return and as she comes round to face he turns under his arm dropping the hand onto his shoulder and so on . . .

To repeat the routine, make sure the man catches with his left hand after the flick spin. Once he has returned the girl, he is on the correct hand to go straight back into the First Move Walk.

Now it's about time to try it with some music!

You have now completed all the moves in the INTERMEDIATE section. If you are happy so far, move on to the advanced routines.

Section 4:
Advanced Routines

Routine 10

(Advanced)

Time to move up to the most accomplished and stylish level! This is the first of three advanced routines in the book and features more complex moves with intriguing names:

Neckbreak Step-Across

Butterfly

Tunnel

Half Nelson

Back Comb Half Catapult

Neckbreak Step-Across Butterfly

The first move in the routine is another variation on the Neckbreak. Start close together, man's left hand to girl's right hand.

1 On the first beat the man makes a small semi-circle with the hands to his left and steps back. As he steps back he signals with his right arm taking it out at right angles to his shoulder, letting  the girl know they are going into a Neckbreak.

2 On the second beat, the man draws the girl forward into his right hand side, gently resting the heel of his right hand on the girl's shoulder. They should now be facing opposite directions.

3 The man takes the girl's right hand and places it in his right hand as he turns her out to the side. The girl should step back on her right foot.

The man should have his right arm resting gently along the girl's shoulders rather than waving around in the air – this will give him more control over the girl and in which direction she moves.

4 The man leads the girl back in, taking hold of her left hand with his left hand as she steps forward on her right foot.

Try to keep this move open, with the girl keeping her head up and shoulders back. The man should try not to pull the girl in too tight and thereby force her to dip her head. Men – be firm but gentle!

5 The man steps to his right, leading with his left hand to bring the girl across in front of him to his left hand side.

6 Now leading with
his right hand,
the man turns
the girl anti-
clockwise as he
takes a quarter
turn to his right
bringing the girl
round behind his
left shoulder.
They are still
double-handed with her right hand in his resting on his
right shoulder.

It is important that the man takes a quarter turn as this
means the girl has less distance to travel as she turns. (If
the man does not turn it is better to allow two beats for
the girl to turn!)

7 The man steps to
his left, leading
the girl across to
the right behind
him, keeping the
hands at shoul-
der height.

This move is
much better if
both partners
look at each other as they step across and smile!

8 The man steps back across to his right, this time leading
the girl across to the left behind him.

This part of the move is called the Butterfly and can be
repeated as often as you like. Men – make sure you step
across too and don't just try to heave your partner across
behind you! The movement for the man is a bit like towelling
your back!

This move can be taken straight into the next move.

Tunnel

1 The man steps
again to his left,
leading the girl
back across to the
right. This time,
as he steps
across, the man
should drop his
right hand to
waist height.

2 The man steps
back to his right,
bringing the girl
back across be-
hind. This time,
however, he
keeps his right
hand low so that
his arm goes be-
hind his back and
he turns slightly

to face the girl as she comes across. There should now
be a loop with the man's arm which the girl can walk
through!

3 Leading with his
left hand the man
pulls down,
drawing the girl
through the loop
made by his arm
to come out be-
hind. As the man
does this he steps
forward to give
the girl more

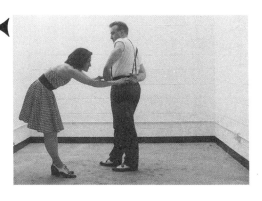

room. The girl needs to crouch down low as she goes
under the man's arm.

4 The man steps
across to his left
and then takes
another step for-
ward as he starts
to lead the girl
back out the
other side.

5 The girl now
comes out to face
on the other side
of the man (his
right). He lets go
with his left hand
and they step
back, coming out
to face, right-to-
right-handed.

This move is really not as difficult as it may seem as long as you remember a couple of essential points . . .

✳ The girl must keep her head ducked down all the way round. Many girls will try to stand up halfway, once they are behind the man and then get stuck trying to come back through. The move will not work if this happens. The girl must keep as low as possible until she has come right back round and out the other side.

✳ The other important thing for this move to work is that **the man must step around the girl.** When you see this move, it appears that the girl is travelling a great distance all the way round the man. In reality, the girl is just stepping forward and back as the man steps around her!

Half Nelson

This is a right-handed move, so start off close together, man's right hand to girl's right hand.

1 On the first beat the man makes a small semi-circle with the hands to his right as they step back.

2 On the second beat, the man steps forward to cut the distance between himself and his partner. He turns himself in an anti-clockwise direction and allows his right hand to go behind his back.

3 The man continues to turn, bending at the waist and ducking as he turns so that he goes under his arm behind his back. To make this move easier, the man can try to sweep the floor with his left hand, which will ensure he is low enough to complete this move successfully.

4 As the man comes round to face he starts to straighten, sweeping up his right hand and taking the girl into a clockwise turn.

5 As the girl completes the turn, the man is now upright facing his partner and they both step back.

Add the Half Nelson to the rest of the routine…

Coming out of the Tunnel the man has got hold of the girl's right hand with his right hand. He is then ready to step straight in and start to turn, ducking down for the Half Nelson.

We have not yet put a return on the Half Nelson as this leads into the start of the final move in this routine.

Back Comb Half Catapult

This is a right-handed move, so start off close together, man's right hand to girl's right hand.

1   On the first beat the man makes a small semi-circle with the hands to his right as they step back and away from each other.

2   On the second beat the man steps in to return the girl taking his hand up above her head as he starts to turn her anti-clockwise.

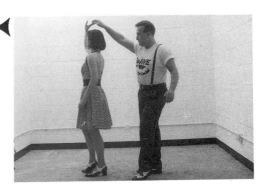

3   As she comes round to face, he dips his hand slightly. He then turns himself clockwise under his own arm to rest his right hand (still holding the girl's hand) on his right shoulder. He now has his back to the girl.

4 The man lets go of the girl's hand and steps forward, dropping his left hand to catch the girl's hand behind. He still has his back to his partner.

The girl should just let her hand slide down the man's back as he steps forward.

5 The man steps back (slightly to his right) as he sweeps his left arm forward and up, pulling the girl through to the front.

6 As she comes through and out to face the man drops the hands and they step back.

Men – be careful not to hit the girl's head as you pull her through to the front – make sure you lift your arm high enough for her to get through!

That's the last move for this routine.

From the Half Nelson into the Back Comb Half Catapult

Coming out of the Half Nelson, the man still has hold of the girl's right hand with his right hand. He steps straight in to return her and as she comes round to face he turns himself under his arm for the Back Comb.

To take it back to the top . . .

As the man steps back after pulling the girl through to face, he should be ready to signal with his right arm for the Neckbreak before drawing the girl straight into his side. Remember – the signal must happen as the man steps back to let the girl know what is happening next. If the man waits to signal as he is already pulling the girl in – **it is too late!**

Now try the whole routine to music!

There are just two more routines to go. Don't worry if you can't remember all the moves we have covered in the book so far, you can always go back to remind yourself! Just remember – the best dancers are not the ones who know hundreds of moves, but the ones who dance fewer moves and dance them properly. Someone who dances cleanly and in time with both the music and their partner will always look better than someone who churns out one move after another but with no precision, style or regard to their partner!

Routine 11
(Advanced)

Nearly there! This routine features complex wraps and turns:

Half Pretzel
Reverse Pretzel
Turning Teapot Walkround
Spin Through
Lean

Half Pretzel

The first move in the routine is a Pretzel variation. Start close together, man's left hand to girl's right hand.

1 On the first beat the man makes a small semi-circle with the hands to his left and steps back. As he steps back, he offers his right hand behind his back, signalling to the girl that this is a Pretzel.

2 Raising his left ◀ hand, the man draws the girl through and she takes hold of his right hand behind his back.

They should now have their backs toward each other.

3 The man drops ◀ his left hand and raises his right as they step across back-to-back.

4 The man lets go with his left hand and starts to turn the girl clockwise.

5 As she comes ◀ round to face he drops the hands and steps back.

They are now in an unusual hand hold with the man holding the girl's left hand with his right.

The Half Pretzel is the perfect lead into the next move . . .

Reverse Pretzel

You are already in the "out" position. The man is holding the girl's left hand in his right hand. To signal the Reverse Pretzel the man takes his left hand and places it behind his back (exactly as before except this time with the left hand).

1 Raising his right hand, the man draws the girl through and she takes hold of his left hand behind his back with her right hand. Again they should have their backs toward each other.

2 The man drops his right hand and raises his left as they step across, back-to-back. The girl has turned to face and the man has formed a loop with his left arm in front of his face.

3 Stepping through that loop the man turns himself clockwise.

4 As the man comes round to face he drops the hands and they step back double-handed.

Practise the two Pretzel variations together. Then try the next move.

Turning Teapot Walkround

Starting from the "out" position, double-handed:

1 The man draws
the girl towards
him taking his
left hand back to
just above his
shoulder.

2 The man keeps
hold with his
right hand as he
pushes with his
left hand to turn the girl clockwise, at the same time
taking a quarter turn to his right.

3 The man drops
his left hand (still
holding the girl's
right) onto the
back of his neck
to check. They
should be side by
side and the girl's
left hand has
now gone behind
her back still
holding the man's right hand.

*You are now in the "Teapot position". To take this into the
Walkround . . .*

4 Keeping in the ◀
Teapot hold,
both step for-
wards, starting
with the right
foot, followed by
the left! (Sounds
obvious but . . .)

Don't try to step
round – just walk
straight forward and you will turn automatically. If you do
try to "step round" you will end up with a "limp" as you walk
which does not look very good. Secondly, if you start with
your left foot you end up dragging your leg round to catch
up which equally does not look good.

Remember each beat is one step with both feet, always
starting with the right.

5 Take another step, starting with the right foot . . .

6 And then a third step which should bring you back to
where you started.

As you walk round, do not stare at the floor! Keep your
head up and look forward – it really looks so much better!

7 The man raises his left hand and brings it over his head
to the front.

8 Leading with his ◀
left hand the man
starts to turn the
girl anti-
clockwise as he
takes a quarter
turn to his right.

9 As the girl comes round to face the man drops his left hand and raises his right continuing to turn the girl anti-clockwise as he takes another quarter turn to his right

10 This time the man drops his right hand onto his shoulder still holding the girl's left hand to check.

You should now be mirroring the original Teapot position with the man's right hand behind his neck holding the girl's left hand and the girl's right arm behind her back holding the man's left hand.

11 Keeping in the Reverse Teapot position, both step forwards, again starting with the right foot, followed by the left!

12 Take another step, starting with the right foot . . .

13 And then a third step which should bring you back again to where you started.

14 The man raises his right hand and brings it over his head to the front.

15 Leading with his ◀
right hand the
man starts to turn
the girl clock-
wise as he takes a
quarter turn to
his left

16 As the girl comes
round to face the
man drops his right hand and raises his left continuing
to turn the girl clockwise as he takes another quarter
turn to his left

17 This time the ◀
man drops his
left hand onto
the back of his
neck still holding
the girl's right
hand to check.

You are now back
in the original
Teapot position.

18 The man lets go of the girl's hand and places his right
hand on her hip to push her away. As they step away
from each other the girl should let her hand slide down
the man's arm to catch right hand to right hand.

**Practise the whole routine so far and – once you are
happy – add on the next move.**

Spin Through

This is a simple move enabling you to change places – and hands if required! Start in the "out" position, man's right to girl's right.

1 The man pulls straight down with his right hand spinning the girl anti-clockwise across in front of him as he steps across to change places.

It is important that the man pulls straight down towards the floor and not out to the side. Ridiculous though it may seem, this lead works! When the man pulls out to the side, he is not giving the girl a clear lead and is actually pulling her off balance. However, when he pulls straight down she has no other option than to follow!

2 As they come out to face having stepped past each other the man catches the girl's right hand with his right hand and they step back.

LEAN

This is the final move in this routine. It's a right-handed move, so start close together, man's right to girl's right.

1 On the first beat the man makes a small semi-circle with the hands to his right and they step back.

2 The man steps in ◄ to return the girl, taking his right hand up above her head as he starts to turn her anti-clockwise.

3 As she comes ◄ round, he turns himself sideways on to her. He takes her hand up over his head and drops her hand onto his right shoulder. He keeps hold of her right hand

with his right hand as he takes his left arm around the girl's waist to lock in this position.

4 The man takes a
big step across
on his right foot,
bending that leg
as he leans to his
right, keeping his
left leg straight
and drawing the
girl in to lean
against him. It

looks better if the girl also raises her left arm, taking it
up in the air rather then just leaving it at her side.

*This should form a good visual line and can be held for
several beats for more dramatic effect if desired!*

5 The man pushes
the girl back into
an upright posi-
tion as he
straightens, us-
ing his right leg to
push himself
back up.

6 With his left
hand on the girl's
waist, and letting
go with his right
hand, the man
pushes her
straight out and
away from him.
He lets her hand
slide down his
arm to catch
man's left hand
to girl's right.

7 The man steps in to return the girl, taking his left hand just up above her head, starting to turn her in an anti-clockwise direction.

8 As the girl comes round to face, the man drops the hands and steps back.

That's the last move for this routine.

Putting it all together . . .

After completing the Spin Through, the man can take the girl straight into a return; he turns himself sideways to bring her into his side to lock, ready for the Lean.

To take it back to the start of the routine, the man must be ready to signal for the Half Pretzel by placing his right hand behind his back as soon as he comes out of the return following the Lean.

You can now repeat this routine as often as you wish. Why not do so to some slow music!

There is just one more routine to complete in this advanced section and, in fact, in the whole book – Good luck!

Routine 12

(Advanced)

This is the final routine in the entire book. It includes some more complex First Move variations, a jump and a drop!

First Move Lock

Seducer

leJIVE Swingout

First Move Jump

Travelling Return

First Move Lock

Start close together, man's left hand to girl's right hand.

1   On the first beat the man makes a small semi-circle with the hands to his left and steps back.

2   On the second beat, the man draws the girl forward into his right hand side, placing his right hand on her waist and she places her left hand on his upper arm. They  should be hip-to-hip, facing opposite directions. (This is the standard First Move position.)

3   The man pushes down and across with his left hand to turn the girl out to the side. As she turns out she should step back on her right foot. The man needs to keep his body position facing forward  and not let it drift round to face his partner.

4 As the man  brings the girl back in, he takes his left hand just above her head to turn her anti-clockwise, keeping his right hand loosely around her waist at all times.

5 As she comes  round to face, the man pulls her in tightly with his right hand on her back to draw her into a standard First Move Lock position. This is similar to the standard First Move hold but the man gives a firm pull with his right hand at the girl's back so she is "locked" in very close.

The man needs to be very careful or he could end up with a black eye while carrying out this move. He must keep his right hand at the girl's waist level and not let it drift higher as she turns! Think about it . . .

From here you can go straight into the next move . . .

Seducer

From the First Move Lock position:

1 The man brings  his right hand up high behind the girl's shoulder. He takes a large step across on his left foot twisting his body round as he lowers the girl down across in front of him, supporting her with his right hand behind her shoulder, whilst holding her right hand in his left.

The man must keep his back straight and bend his knees to lose height. He should not lean over otherwise he may go off balance and drop his partner or hurt his own back. In all moves involving lowering and raising your partner the man must never use his back to lift – a back injury is painful, can affect your working life and could even stop you from dancing permanently. Use your arms, shoulders and leg muscles.

2 To come back
up, the man just straightens his legs, still keeping his back straight to bring the girl up and back into the First Move Lock position. He supports her back with his right hand and pulls with his left as he raises her up.

For a more dramatic effect, this move can be held in the drop position for a couple of beats. It is also a good one to finish on!

leJIVE Swingout

You can go into this move from the First Move Lock hold:
Start in the First Move position, hip-to-hip with the man's
right hand on the girl's waist and the girl's left hand on the
man's arm.

1 The man pushes
down with his
left hand to turn
the girl out to the
side. She should
step back on her
right foot. The
man's left hand
should be kept at
waist level and
his right hand on
the small of the girl's back.

2 The man brings
the girl forward
again, so that she
steps in on her
right foot. He
keeps his left
hand low, to
"sandwich" her
with his right
hand on her back
and his left hand
bringing her right hand across her front.

3 The man steps back using his right hand on the girl's back to push her away so that she blocks against her own arm, facing away from him. The girl should keep her left arm out of the way so that it does not get trapped against her other arm. (It looks good if she holds it high in the air.)

4 Stepping back, the man gives a firm pull with his left hand to twist the girl back round to face.

This move needs a lot of tension between the two partners for it to work.

Try linking the routine together so far. You should find that once they are put together, each move will flow quite naturally into the next.

First Møve Jump

The next move in this final routine is the First Move Jump. Before going into this move you should be aware of several things:

✳ **Firstly, this is a "jump" – not a lift or a throw.** The man does not need to be incredibly strong to do this move!

✳ **This move has a clear signal.** Any moves like this should not be carried out if the girl does not recognise the signal. Likewise, the girl should not attempt to lead this move herself and jump, if the man does not indicate with a signal.

✳ **If you are dancing on a crowded dance floor, do not attempt a move like this – it needs a lot of space. You will not only risk hurting yourselves but also other dancers around you.** *The man must check to see where the girl will land before taking her into a jump.*

This is a left-handed move, so start off close together, man's left hand to girl's right hand.

1 On the first beat ◀ the man makes a small semi-circle with the hands to his left as they step back and away from each other. The man signals this move by placing his right hand on his right shoulder, tapping it once.

> Remember – if the girl does not know the signal, do not attempt this move. Similarly, if the man does not signal this move, girls do not jump.

2 The man now draws the girl in to his right hand side so they are standing hip-to-hip as for a standard First Move. However, this time the man ensures that he tightens his hold  with his left hand on the girl's right hand.

It is essential that the man keeps a firm grip with his left hand otherwise as the girl comes out of the move there is a strong chance that she will fall as she lands.

3 On the third beat the man pushes down with his left hand turning the girl out to the side. She takes a step back on her right foot and bends her knees preparing to jump. At this  point the man moves his right arm around the girl's waist so that he has a firm hold of his partner with the right hand. The girl places her left hand on the man's shoulder for extra support.

4 Keeping a firm  hold with his left hand and using his right around her waist the man guides the girl round to the front as she jumps.

It is important to note that the girl just jumps up and the man just guides her round. The girl does not need to jump a long way, neither does the man need to lift her.

5 As the girl comes  round the man releases his hold with his right arm at her waist so that she lands in front of him in the "out" position, still holding left-to-right.

To make this move look more dramatic the girl should bend her knees as she jumps. This does not mean she will be any higher but it gives the impression that she is further away from the ground!

Adding the jump to the rest of the routine:

As the man pulls the girl round to face, coming out of the *le*JIVE Swingout, he should pat his right shoulder with his right hand to signal the First Move Jump. He can then draw the girl straight in to prepare for the jump.

To give the girl time to regain her balance we will just repeat one of the moves from Routine 4, before going back to the top.

Travelling Return

Start in the "out" position with the man's left hand holding the girl's right hand.

1 The man simply draws the girl forward, leading with his left hand just slightly above and in front of her head, as he steps forward too.

2 As the girl walks forward, she will get so far until she cannot walk any further and will automatically turn herself out to face. They have both now changed places.

That's the very last move for this routine, this section and indeed for the whole book –

the only thing left to do now is dance and enjoy!

So take it from the very top, with some music.

After eight . . . .

Index of Moves

More Great Music – Special Offer!

If you enjoyed the free sampler CD with this book, you can get a full-length Modern Jive CD by the same musicians with 9 more tracks that are excellent for dancing. **START TO DANCE MODERN JIVE** retails at £9.99 but readers can order direct from us for just £7.95 *POST FREE!*

The tracks are: **My Baby Just Cares For Me** (originally recorded by Nina Simone) **Runaround Sue** (originally recorded by Dion & The Belmonts) **You Never Can Tell** (originally recorded by Chuck Berry) **Can't Help Myself** (originally recorded by The Four Tops) **Crocodile Rock** (originally recorded by Elton John) **Crazy Little Thing Called Love** (originally recorded by Queen) **Tainted Love** (originally recorded by Soft Cell) **Love Shack** (originally recorded by The B52s) **Rhythm Is A Dancer** (originally recorded by Snap) **Move It On Up** (originally recorded by M People) **U got 2 Let The Music** (originally recorded by Capella) **(I) Just Can't Get Enough** (originally recorded by Transformer 2)

Sigma Leisure, 1 South Oak Lane, Wilmslow, Cheshire SK9 6AR
Phone: 01625 – 531035 Fax: 01625 – 536800   E-mail: sigma.press@zetnet.co.uk
VISA and Mastercard welcome.   Free Catalogue.   Internet: www.sigmapress.co.uk

Britain's Hottest Dance Phenomenon!

leJIVE run classes and events throughout the country
COME ALONG - it's fun, friendly and you don't need to bring a partner

leJIVE Classes
All classes start with a class designed for absolute beginner's. This is then followed by an intermediate class and then at least an hour of "freestyle" dancing so you can meet new people and practice the moves you've learnt

leJIVE Events
Almost every weekend there are events often with live music - great evenings, great atmosphere - **IT'S WHY YOU LEARNT TO DANCE!**

leJIVE, leVIDEO
20 moves, clearly demonstrated by Robert Austin and Claire Hilliard
Available from all good video outlets

leJIVE on the Internet
Up to the minute information on all aspects of leJIVE, including animated moves
- THE GROUND BREAKING VIRTUAL DANCE SITE. http://www.lejive.com

leJIVE Promotions
Parties, Theme nights, Corporate Functions. Put a swing into your next event!

UK Modern Jive Open
Britain's largest freestyle jive competition. A whole day of dancing with the best dancers from across the country competing for large cash prizes, trophies and national titles - an event not to be missed. Held around the first week in October every year

TEACHERS AND FRANCHISEES
leJIVE is opening new classes all across the country on a regular basis - we need teachers and franchisees to help us expand. We provide full training and support
FOR FURTHER INFORMATION CONTACT: leJIVE, UNIT 1T, LEROY HOUSE, 436 ESSEX ROAD, LONDON N1 3QP. Tel: 0171 359 2800; Fax: 0171 354 5793